1%

This item was
purchased with
monies provided
from the optional
1% sales tax.

THE WARLORD'S MESSENGERS

The WARLORD'S MESSENGERS

BY VIRGINIA WALTON PILEGARD

ILLUSTRATED BY
NICOLAS DEBON

PELICAN PUBLISHING COMPANY
GRETNA 2005

Library of Congress Cataloging-in-Publication Data

Pilegard, Virginia Walton.
  The warlord's messengers / by Virginia Walton Pilegard ; illustrated
by Nicolas Debon.
      p. cm.
  Summary: In ancient China, Chuan and Jing Jing invent a cart that
sails on land in order to quickly reach the warlord with an important
message from the emperor.
  ISBN-13: 978-1-58980-271-1 (alk. paper)
  [1. Inventions—Fiction. 2. Travel—Fiction. 3. China—History—
Fiction.] I. Debon, Nicolas, ill. II. Title.

  PZ7.P6283Waqm 2005
  [E]—dc22
                                2004031084

Printed in Singapore
Published by Pelican Publishing Company, Inc.
1000 Burmaster Street, Gretna, Louisiana 70053

THE WARLORD'S MESSENGERS

Many years ago in China, a young boy named Chuan lived in the palace of an important warlord. One day he saw a messenger arrive at the palace carrying a scroll stamped with the emperor's royal seal. Excited rumors spread among the palace servants. The emperor's message demanded their warlord's attendance at a banquet for all the empire's military governors in *just fourteen days*.

"My master is not here," said the warlord's steward. His voice betrayed his dismay.

"Where is he?" asked the messenger.

"Three days' journey to the north," answered the steward.

The messenger stretched his weary shoulders. "I have already traveled ten difficult days from the city of the emperor to this place."

"This is not good," muttered the steward. "It will take three more days to ride to my master's camp. It will take him three days to ride back here. Three days plus three days equals six days. Another ten days from this palace to the city of the emperor adds up to sixteen days. My master will be two days late—a grave dishonor."

Still clutching the scroll, the messenger placed his foot in the stirrup and swung onto his horse. "That is no problem of mine. My only task is to personally deliver the message to your master." He turned the horse to walk in the direction of the warlord's camp.

"It would be a terrible thing for our master to be late to the emperor's feast." The steward wrung his hands. "All the other military governors would arrive first. They would receive favor with the emperor. Our master will be shamed."

Chuan turned to see his friend Jing Jing, the puppet master's daughter, standing at his side. "If the message is so important, why is the emperor's messenger allowing his horse to walk? Should he not gallop?" she asked.

"A man who tries to gallop a horse all day will find himself walking," said the steward.

"So what is faster than a horse?" she wondered aloud.

"On the river where I once lived," said Chuan, "boats traveled faster than the wind."

Jing Jing smiled. "Because the wind breathed into their sails."

"If only one could use the wind to travel by land." Chuan watched the leaves stir on the trees in the palace garden.

ing Jing began to hop up and down with excitement. "We could harness the wind if we attached a sail to my father's cart!"

It was not easy for the children to convince Jing Jing's father to lend them his cart. It was not easy for them to persuade the warlord's steward to let them use the sail from the warlord's boat. And it was not easy to attach the sail to the cart. But when Chuan and Jing Jing had accomplished these three things, they set out to test their new invention.

A brisk wind filled their sail and whisked them along so quickly that the cart wheels barely touched the ground. Before they knew it, the wind carried them north toward the warlord's camp.

"I did not know human beings could go so fast!" Jing Jing shouted.

"We forgot to invent a way to stop!" Chuan yelled back.

"The wind will die down sometime," said Jing Jing, who discovered she loved to ride with her hair blowing and the roadside flashing by.

They soon learned to guide the cart by adjusting the sail as they hurtled by bushes and rocks.

"Look! Look! There is the messenger resting by the side of the road." Chuan pointed in the distance.

"We can't stop!" Chuan yelled to the messenger as they approached. "Throw us the scroll."

"I will not entrust the emperor's important business to children!" the messenger shouted as Chuan and Jing Jing sped by. His frightened horse reared at the sight of a wind-sailing cart, then whirled and fled.

The children looked back to see the messenger throw his hat on the ground and stomp on it before he ran down the road after the horse.

On and on they raced.

"I see the warlord and his men!" Chuan cried.
"Help! Stop us!" he and Jing Jing shouted.

"Hold on!" the warlord bellowed. He and his men stretched a hemp rope across the road.

The sailing cart hit the rope and the mast snapped. The cart shuddered to a stop.

"Sir," Chuan hurried to say, "behind us on the road is a messenger with an invitation for you from the emperor."

The warlord studied the cart with its broken mast.

"You must be in the emperor's city in fourteen days," Chuan declared, eager for the warlord to understand the urgency of the message.

"When did you leave the palace?" the warlord asked.

"Today at midday," Chuan said.

The warlord looked down at the shadows cast at his feet by the afternoon sun. "It cannot be more than three hours past midday now," he murmured. "I saw how fast your sailing cart flew, but you want me to believe you traveled in three hours a distance that would have taken my horse three ten-hour days?" The warlord shook his head.

"We had to deliver the message," Jing Jing said. "We couldn't allow our warlord to be dishonored."

"Ah yes, the invitation." The warlord scowled. "How do I know you children tell the truth about this message?"

"You can ask the emperor's messenger. I'm sure you will meet him along the way," Chuan said.

"Two days back," Jing Jing added. Her eyes shone with laughter.

"If you begin for your palace first thing tomorrow, on horseback," Chuan said, "you will arrive at the city of the emperor with one day to spare."

"**I** will start back with my men." The warlord pointed his finger at Chuan. "If this is a trick, young Chuan, you and your father and the puppet master and his family will all be driven from my palace."

One of the warlord's men harnessed the cart behind his horse. The children traveled in silence, sure they would meet the emperor's messenger soon. By the second day, they began to worry.

"He must have lost some time catching his horse," Jing Jing remarked.

At last they glimpsed the hatless messenger, riding toward them.

When the warlord read the message, he turned to Chuan and Jing Jing. "You have told me the truth and your cleverness has saved me from dishonor. This is the proper time for you to meet the emperor. I'm sure he will want to meet children who can make a cart travel ten times as fast as a horse."

Chuan and Jing Jing bowed in awe at the thought of such an important meeting. As they began the journey, they could hardly contain their excitement. They could only imagine the adventures awaiting them in the city of the emperor.

You may have guessed that land sailing is a Chinese invention. The *Book of the Golden Hall Master*, written around A.D. 550, mentions a wind-driven carriage that carried thirty men and traveled several hundred li in a day. One li equals one-half kilometer or three-tenths of a mile. Sixteenth-century Western writers marveled that China's sailing carriages reached speeds of thirty to forty miles per hour. Our story uses the English measurement "hours" and a wind-carriage speed of thirty miles per hour. The warlord and Chuan would have measured time in *shi'chen,* or two-hour intervals, and distance in li.

To make your own windsock (also a Chinese invention) and estimate how fast Chuan's land-sailing cart would travel today:

1.
Cut off the end of a cylindrical oatmeal box.

2.
Measure and cut a piece of cloth (such as an old pillowcase) two times the length of the oatmeal box and wide enough to go around its circumference.

3.
Glue the cloth around the box so that half the cloth hangs free below the open end of the box. Cut streamers from the bottom of the cloth to the bottom of the box.

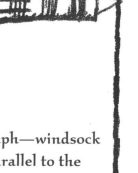

4.
Punch four holes near the top of the box to fasten strings to hang your windsock.

A land-sailing vehicle is able to travel three times the speed of the wind and sails best in wind velocities of ten miles per hour and above. Check the wind scale for your windsock below, multiply that speed by three, and you will have the corresponding cart speed.

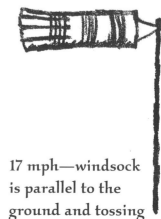

Wind Scale:

0 mph—windsock hangs limp

6 mph—windsock is partly lifted, sloping thirty degrees from the ground

12 mph—windsock is lifted roughly parallel to the ground

17 mph—windsock is parallel to the ground and tossing against the strings